Goodness, for God's Sake

Sound Teaching, Sensible Living, and Good Deeds
from Paul's Letter to Titus

Christine Schneider

ECS
MINISTRIES
The Word to the World

Goodness, for God's Sake: Sound Teaching, Sensible Living, and Good Deeds from Paul's Letter to Titus
copyright 2004 by ECS Ministries

Published by ECS Press
ECS Ministries, Dubuque, IA 52001
www.ecsministries.org

Cover and text design by Gregory C. Benoit Publishing
Old Mystic, CT 06372

www.gregwa.com

ISBN 1-59387-005-1

All scripture quotations, unless otherwise indicated, are taken from the New American Standard Bible (NASB), copyright the Lockman Foundation 1960, 1962, 1963, 1968, 1971, 1972, 1973, 1975, 1977. All rights reserved.

Contents

Kitchen Table Studies

Bible Studies for Women

"Why don't you stop by for coffee?"

You've just dropped the kids off for school, or you've run into a friend at the grocery store. The invitation to come for coffee communicates such an easy companionship. You are not being invited to a meal with all the attendant preparations and deadlines. You do not need to change your clothes or bring flowers. Whether the coffee is served in fine china cups or in a hodge-podge of garage sale mugs, the emphasis is on the relationship. "Why don't you stop by for coffee?" is in invitation to informality, yet it is also an open door to discuss more important things than the weather.

Neither of you needs the coffee nor the store-bought cookies planned for just such an occasion. What you need is the comfortable camaraderie, catching up on events gone by or continuing a conversation put on hold by the daily busyness of our lives. You won't stay long; the laundry is calling your name, and the dishwasher needs to be loaded. Yet, this little visit is an oasis of calm in your busy day. Back home you will sense the strength gained by the time spent lingering over a cup of coffee with a friend.

In Proverbs 31:26, we read that the excellent wife "opens her mouth in wisdom, and the teaching of kindness is on her tongue." Since her number one priority seems to be her home and family, I believe her teaching occurs within this context. Kitchen Table Studies are designed to help you to develop strong relationships both with other women and with your God.

Unlike instant coffee, there is no instant formula for loving and obeying God. This only occurs as you soak your mind and heart in God's living Word. There is also no shortcut to growing friendships with other women. We need to spend time with one another, sharing things we have in common and encouraging one another to live as we ought to live. Then our friendships will deepen. We will become the shoulder on which our friends may lean in their times of trouble, and they will become our encouragement to live each day to please God.

Kitchen Table Studies will be most effective if you study with one or more friends. Each session is broken up into four parts. The first part introduces at least one of the truths you will meet in the passage you will be studying.

The leader of your study might want to read or refer to this opening before plunging into God's Word.

The second section, *Discover God's Truth*, is the heart of your Bible study. The questions are not numbered sequentially (1, 2, 3, etc.) but simply according to the verse numbers in the Scripture passage. This is to emphasize that you are studying God's Word in an orderly fashion within its context to find out what it means, rather than hunting for verses to support a concept. In your group it would be helpful if all the women first answer the questions at home. Then, when you meet, each one can read a question, give her answers, and allow others to contribute additional thoughts. I have tried to keep cross-references to a minimum for they are time consuming in a group Bible study. Your study leader, however, may decide to have you look up a few during your time together.

At the end of the study section I have written a wrap-up, summarizing what you will have learned about the main passage. After your own study is completed, I hope that my train of thought will now seem obvious. In the group time you can usually skip this part entirely, for you will already have covered the information thoroughly.

The last section is called *Make Truth Personal*. The reason God's Word changes us is that we pour it into our brains and then it trickles down into our hearts and lives. Now you will move what you have learned from "Bible times" into the present day. You will take the knowledge you have gained and figure out how it relates to you. These questions are more personal—hopefully, life-changing. This is where you will get to know the other women in the study better, as you encourage one another to live according to the truths you have learned.

In a group, there may be a few women who are not ready to share their answers to every question. The leader can open up the questions to the whole group, and be prepared to share some of her own applications, humbly demonstrating God's work in her life.

You will come across the phrase *Pause to Pray* interspersed throughout each lesson. This is an invitation to you, as a group, to pause and reflect upon what you have just discussed and talk to God about it in prayer. You may be filled with praise, reassured by a promise, convicted about a sin, confronted by a weakness, or startled by God's solution to a problem. We are forgetful creatures. Before you forget that precious, enlightening truth, talk to God about it, and even note down your thoughts. Then continue with the study.

Suggestions for Leading a Kitchen Table Study

To get the maximum benefits from Kitchen Table Studies you should probably plan on spending two hours together. When the women first arrive, the hostess should offer light refreshments and allow time for some "visiting" before settling down to the study. A big table is a great location; it is so much easier to lay your Bible, this study guide, and a coffee mug on a flat surface, rather than to try to juggle them on your lap. The following format is one suggestion to guide you in completing each Bible study.

1. After you welcome everyone, gather prayer requests. Limit the time for sharing so you have time to pray! One practice that saves time is for the person with a request to not *tell* about it, but be the one to *pray* about it. In so doing the other ladies learn of the need via the prayer itself, and may add their "amens" to it. Ask someone to keep a list and to print it up for everyone for the following week. Rotate dated requests on and off the list.

2. Spend some time in prayer, encouraging those who would like to pray aloud to cover these requests and ask for God's guidance for the whole Bible study time.

3. Begin your study. Give each woman a chance to read a question and share her answer. Let everyone know that if they don't have the answer, they may still read a question and attempt to answer it, or they may ask the others what answer they have. Try to keep moving. You can graciously avoid "rabbit trails" by saying, "That's an interesting question (or thought). Let's finish up here and then perhaps we'll have time to discuss this afterwards." If you don't know the answer to a question, just say so, and determine how the group will find it out.

4. When you come to *Pause to Pray*, give the women 30 seconds or so to reflect on the previous section and then ask someone to pray aloud on that topic.

At the end of the Bible study, wrap up your time in prayer. This prayer time should be focused upon what the women have learned from the Scripture passage for their lives. Pray for the desire to obey, the strength to stand up in trials, and the courage to do what is right. May this quality time produce friendships with God and with others that will spiritually nourish your mind and life!

Goodness, for God's Sake

Goodness, for God's Sake

Sound Teaching, Sensible Living, and Good Deeds
from Paul's Letter to Titus

> There was a little girl, who had a little curl,
> Right in the middle of her forehead,
> And when she was good, she was very, very good,
> But when she was bad, she was horrid.
>
> —Mother Goose

Even before we're old enough to lisp this poem, people are telling us to be good.

"If you're good, you may have a cookie."

"Oh, you're such a good girl!"

"I'll try to be good."

As we grow older, being good becomes harder and harder. Our thoughts, motives, and attitudes get in the way. If we're honest, we know that just *doing* good things—while it might earn us praise from parents and teachers—is not the same as *being* good. Besides, it is simply impossible to be good enough. Some of us give up. We become the rebel in the family, the terror of the schoolyard, the black sheep. Others try harder, despised by siblings and classmates as boring, Miss Goody-two-shoes, hypocrite.

Hypocrite: A religious word that brings up another problem. God. Any knowledge of God at all suggests that He is bigger and more powerful than we are, and that He is completely different than we are. And we know how we are: small, weak, frustrated by imperfections, and sometimes just horrid. Good sense tells us that we either need to keep Him at a distance or appease Him. Yet being good enough to please God seems as impossible as keeping Him away. He can see right through us. Those pesky thoughts, motives and attitudes contaminate almost every good thing we do.

This puts us in a dilemma, for the Bible is full of commands to obey, instructions to follow, and encouragement to do good to others. We suspect that God is not fooled by good behavior mixed with bad motives and attitudes. Good deeds can't even erase a traffic violation. So why does God make a big deal about being good? And why do some people believe that good deeds pave the way to heaven?

The little book of Titus reveals insights into God's reasoning. Pleasing God is really not as difficult as we make it. *We just have to be rightly related to Him.* Once we are, He enables us to please Him. Come with us to visit the New Testament church on Crete and discover how true goodness is not only necessary, but possible. This is goodness for God's sake.

Session One
Faith that Molds Character

Overview of Paul's Letter to Titus

September 11, 2001. Your world has changed because of the events that occurred that day. Eleven Muslim men hijacked four jet airplanes, and in the resulting catastrophes the lives of over three thousand men, women, and children were snuffed out. Their motivation? Religious zeal.

Religion can be dangerous. Stephen was a young man who loved the Lord Jesus Christ. Everywhere he went he radiated grace and confidence. He was compassionate and served the poorest of the poor with humility. The Christians in Jerusalem esteemed him so highly that they appointed him, along with just five other godly men, to a very responsible position in the young church. Those who were not Christians, however, did not like him, for he preached against their traditional beliefs. Because they were a part of the "establishment," strength was on their side. When it finally came to a confrontation Stephen won the verbal battle, but his opponents raged against the obvious truth. That rage turned murderous.

Another young man, one of the religious leaders' most promising students, watched Stephen's murder take place. Saul took no part in Stephen's execution, but he was in complete agreement with it. He heard how the young preacher skillfully proved from the Holy Scriptures that Jesus of Nazareth was the Messiah—and not only the Messiah, but God's Son, God in the flesh!

Blasphemy! This new religion had to be stopped. If some of the religious leaders wanted to get rid of Stephen, Saul was not going to stop them. Perhaps Saul had a cooler head than most; he minded the cloaks of those who picked up rocks and bludgeoned young Stephen to a pulp.

That day changed Jerusalem. The devout Jews began a systematic search for all of the Nazarene's followers. There were thousands of them, and they fled from the capital city into all corners of the Roman Empire. Saul, however, was a man of vision, and he knew that the sect would eventually return to Jerusalem if it were allowed to flourish in even the remotest provinces. He became one of Judaism's staunchest defenders and the church's worst enemy. If the Christians did not flee, Saul dragged them from their homes and put them into prison.

Decades later this same man traveled the dusty roads of the Roman Empire preaching that Jesus was the Christ, and he suffered much persecution as a result. He would become the man who wrote such comforting words as "We proved to be gentle among you [the believers in Thessalonica]" (1 Thessalonians 2:7) and "We have peace with God, through our Lord Jesus Christ." (Romans 5:1). What could change this angry, zealous, proud Jew into the apostle Paul, the man who wrote most of our New Testament?

Discover God's Truth

This first lesson will differ from those that follow; we are beginning with an overview of the book of Titus.

Read the whole of Titus five times, that is, for five days in a row if possible. With your readings, complete the following elements.

First Reading: Read the book straight through. Afterwards, jot down a few thoughts or impressions that stick with you.

Second Reading: As you read, note some significant words that keep popping up. Write them below.

Third Reading: Before you read, look up the following words in a regular dictionary. Write the definitions in your glossary at the back of this study book.

Good/Goodness:

Faith/Belief:

Works/Deeds:

Doctrine/Teaching:

Fourth Reading: Again, get out your dictionary and look up these words, completing your glossary as you go. Then read through.

Grace:

Truth:

Hope:

Sensible: (Your version may say "self controlled." Look up both words.)

Fifth Reading: After this last reading, write down any questions you have. Ten weeks from now, when you are finishing this study, we will come back to this page and see how many answers you have found.

ꗞ Pause to Pray ꗞ

Ask God to reveal many practical truths from Titus to you and the
other ladies with whom you are studying.

After Paul became a Christian, he later described to the believers at Philippi
what his life was like before he was saved (Philippians 3:5–7). He described his
background, perfect in the eyes of the Jewish nation. From his birth, he was
a "Hebrew of Hebrews." His parents followed the Jewish law exactly, making
sure they did everything right for their son. They named him Saul, after Israel's
first king—the tallest, best-looking man in the country. They circumcised him
on his eighth day of life, and then when he grew up they made sure he was
educated to be a Pharisee. His life was completely in accord with everything
required by the Jewish religion. He was a Jew, one of God's chosen people. He
kept the law so rigidly that even on trial he would have been found blameless
of any wrong. He was so Jewish, in fact, that he defended his religion against
the dangerous new sect of the Christians. He persecuted them mercilessly,
because he was totally committed to the Jewish religion. Tolerance had no
place in his life when heresy threatened what he believed to be the truth.

It would take something earthshaking to change his mind. So God, who
is great in mercy, and who needed a committed man to spearhead His plans
to grow the church, shook Saul's earth. In Acts 9:1–2 we read that Saul was
"breathing threats and murder against the disciples" of Jesus Christ. He went
to the high priest and asked for permission to search out the Christians who
had fled from Jerusalem. It was necessary to stamp out this sect quickly and
completely. The Christians could not be allowed to spread their "heresy" to
other parts of the world. The high priest gave Saul the letters and sent him
first to Damascus, Syria, to bring Christians, both men and women, bound,
back to Jerusalem.

God, however, had other plans (Acts 9:3–19). As Saul and his men came
near to Damascus, a light from heaven suddenly flashed around Saul, and he
fell to the ground. He heard a Voice say, "Saul, Saul, why are you persecuting
Me?"

Saul seemed to know that God was speaking, as he asked, "Who are you,
Lord?"

The Voice answered, "I am Jesus, whom you are persecuting. Now get up and go into the city, and you will be told what you must do" (Acts 9:5-6).

Having been literally blinded by the light, Saul had to be led by his men into the city. There he met Ananias, the man God had prepared to heal his eyes and also lay hands on him to signal his being filled with the Holy Spirit. Now he had spiritual sight, too.

Saul's conversion changed his life. For the next several days the understandably skeptical Christians listened to Saul testifying in public that Jesus was God's Son. Before his time in Damascus was over, they were convinced that this former murderous Pharisee was, indeed, one of them. Suddenly, he became a target for all the hatred he had once spewed out toward the Christians. With a plot afoot to kill him, the believers smuggled him out of the city.

They sent him to Jerusalem, where Barnabas took him under his wing and helped Saul convince the apostles that his conversion was genuine. His former extensive knowledge of the Old Testament Scriptures now made him almost impossible to refute. This time, Hellenistic Jews (Gentiles who had converted to Judaism) wanted to kill him, so he escaped to Tarsus, his hometown, located in present-day Turkey.

Paul gives us a glimpse into the next phase of his life in Galatians 1:11–2:10. To prepare him for his unique assignment in Christian history, God led him to spend the next three years receiving direct teaching from God concerning new doctrines and evangelism. Ironically, the man who was raised and educated to be the perfect Jew became the man who would step away from Judaism and be a missionary to non-Jews. Soon he would convince the other apostles to draw a line of separation between Judaism and Christianity.

Of course, it is important to remember our salvation heritage. The shadows of our salvation are there in the Old Testament. As believers, we should be students of both the Old and New Testaments, recognizing, as Jesus told the Samaritan woman that "salvation is from the Jews" (John 4:22).

For Saul, however, God charged him with teaching the Gentile world that salvation through Jesus was available to all, without having to become a Jew.

Eventually, Saul, who was now using his Roman (Gentile) given name of Paul (meaning "small, insignificant"), was sent out by one of the churches in Asia Minor to be the first missionary (Acts 13:1–5). He and his fellow workers journeyed by foot through the Middle East, Asia Minor, and southern Europe, spreading the good news of salvation through Jesus Christ wherever they went. They baptized new converts, started churches, and trained and appointed leaders. The zeal that had once motivated him to defend the Jewish faith from Christians now gave him the energy to preach and teach that once-hated message. Acts 13–28 follows Paul's story.

Christian tradition, not Scripture, tells us of the end of Paul's life. After going to Rome as a prisoner, Paul spent several years there under house arrest. During that time, he wrote many of the letters we have in our New Testament. When Paul finally went to trial, he appeared before Emperor Nero, whose evil had not yet fully developed. Nero let him go. The book of Titus was most likely written during this time. A few years later, both Peter and Paul were arrested and tried. According to tradition they were both executed; Peter, the apostle to the Jews, was crucified upside-down; Paul, the apostle to the Gentiles, was beheaded.

Make Truth Personal

You will have already noticed how often Paul mentions the importance of sound teaching, sensible living, and good works. As we study the book of Titus, watch for evidences of how each one seems to build on the other.

1. Paul didn't quit being a Jew when he became a believer in Jesus Christ. What changes did take place, according to Philippians 3:4–8?

2. If you are a Christian, what changes have occurred in your life that would convince others that your faith is genuine? How have you grown spiritually?

If you are not yet sure you are a Christian, what changes would you like to see in your life?

3. What changes in your life do you suspect the Holy Spirit may speak to you about before this Bible study is completed?

🕊 Pause to Pray 🕊

Confess any hard-heartedness you have that could hinder God's Spirit from getting through to you in this study of Titus. Ask Him for a teachable heart.

If your faith is genuine, it will change your goals, your deeds, and your character—probably in that order.

Notes

Session Two
Ambassador Of Hope

Titus 1:1-4

Appointing ambassadors is a very important priority for a country. While my husband and I lived in Austria, we were fascinated to watch United States' ambassadors come and go. No doubt the President of the u.s. had little problem finding eager volunteers to move to "gemuetliche" Vienna, Austria. Who wouldn't want to live on the banks of the beautiful blue Danube River! It was probably no accident that the ambassadors were usually women. But as charming as the country is, it is still a foreign culture, and some of the diplomats quickly became disenchanted with the job.

My husband and I, fluent in German, at ease in the culture, and in love with the Austrian people, sometimes joked about our own suitability for the job—until we really got to thinking about what an ambassador's role entails.

The United States' ambassador to Austria protects and represents the best interests of the u.s. to the Austrians. The ambassador takes her orders from the President of the u.s. An effective ambassador will never become an Austrian citizen, and she will always put the priorities of the u.s. before the welfare of Austria. She is not worried about what the Austrians think of her; her loyalty is directed only to her own President.

Naturally, exercising some basic courtesies helps to foster a friendly relationship between two such countries. If the ambassador learns the language and tries to understand and appreciate the culture, she will be less likely to unnecessarily offend the members of the Austrian government. If she enjoys their food, learns their history, and loves their people, she will be able to make decisions that will be mutually beneficial to both governments.

In the end, however, the ambassador is responsible to her own President. His ambassadors are to please him. They are to complete his agenda. They are sent to other countries to do his will. If the Austrians would like to work with him, they can do it through the ambassador, in the way the ambassador suggests. If they do not agree with the President's priorities, it is still the ambassador's job to communicate her President's will, even if, in doing so, she damages her relationship to her host country.

As a preparation for this Bible study, look through newspapers and magazines, or listen to television or radio news, and list the different kinds of bad things that happen to people. Write down the feelings (whether recorded or not) of people who are victims of crimes, disasters, and scandals.

Discover God's Truth

Read Titus 1:1–4. Although Paul addresses his letter to Titus, it was to the church on Crete that he was establishing his authority, as it was important that the people listen to Titus. Paul was God's ambassador (2 Corinthians 5:20), and Titus was his delegated authority.

In Titus 1:1, Paul claims to be a bondservant of God. The actual connotation of this word is "slave." We don't like to think of ourselves as slaves, for slaves are not masters of their own destiny. Paul, however, used this idea to highlight his commitment to God and his desire to serve God forever.

For background, read from another of Paul's writings, Romans 6:17–18. What two kinds of slavery are mentioned here?

Can a person be a slave of both of these?

When does a person become a slave of sin? How long does that last?

When does a person become a slave of righteousness? How long does this slavery last?

Who has freed us? What part does obedience from the heart play? Look up Romans 5:8 for help.

What is the slave's responsibility to his or her master? How much say does the slave has in what he or she will or won't do?

How does all this apply to Paul in Titus 1:1?

Paul also stated he was an *apostle*. Look up the word in a dictionary and add the definition to your glossary. What is the root definition? What other definitions are applicable?

How does that apply to Paul?

In Acts 1:21–22, as the eleven disciples are choosing someone to replace Judas Iscariot, they decide on requirements for being considered an apostle: (1) a follower of Jesus; (2) one who was present for Jesus' whole ministry; (3) a witness of Jesus' resurrection and ascension.

Paul, of course, did not meet all of these, so he explains his apostleship in 1 Corinthians 15:7–9: "Then [Jesus] appeared to James, then to all the apostles; and last of all, as it were to one untimely born, He appeared to me also. For I am the least of the apostles, who am not fit to be called an apostle, because I persecuted the church of God." Most biblical scholars agree that the risen Lord Himself appeared to Paul, preventing him from carrying out his persecution toward the Damascus Christians.

v. 1: To what purpose was Paul sent?

Whose faith was Paul supporting? What would Paul's description of believers here have meant to his Cretan readers?

What is the relationship between faith and knowledge?

Which one comes first in our spiritual life?

What is the result of exercising faith in the knowledge of the truth?

v. 2: What motivates Paul to continue, even when the "foreign culture" of this ungodly world becomes too much for him? Notice the main verbs and when they happen.

> . . . in the hope of eternal life
>   which God . . . .   promised
>   who cannot lie   long ages ago
>   BUT
>   (which God). . . . . manifested
>   at the proper time

Perhaps you became a Christian later in life. Write down what your life was like before and after salvation, especially in regard to hope for your future. If you were very young or you're not sure, ask someone you know who became a Christian as an adult to share her testimony. Share here what she said about her previous hopelessness, her present hope, and how it helps her live.

✺ Pause to Pray ✺

Praise God for new life in Christ!

---

v. 3: What was the core of the message that Paul's Lord wanted him to communicate?

Where did he get his message to pass along?

Think about the proclamations and commands that a President issues. How important are they to the President himself? To the ambassador?

v. 4: Paul calls Titus his true son in their common faith. Because Paul was a Jew and Titus a Greek, the faith they had in common was their saving faith in Jesus Christ. Titus seems to have worked in Corinth for a while (2 Corinthians 7:6–7; 8:16, 23). We do not know how long Paul and Titus worked among the believers on Crete before Paul left. Paul obviously had confidence that Titus would love and care for them just as Paul would, had it been possible for him to complete his mission there.

What do you think "his true child" in the faith means? (What was Paul and Titus's relationship?)

Some Christians simply warm the pews on Sunday mornings. They are very careful not to ruffle too many feathers. They justify their passiveness by saying they don't want to "turn people off" by how they express their faith. They don't want to be associated with "fanatics" that give Christianity a bad name, so they do their best to keep their beliefs very quiet. After all, faith is "personal."

Paul was not such a Christian. Having been called, he served God publicly and wholeheartedly. He recognized that the price paid for him was so dear that serving his Good Master for the rest of his days was the only appropriate thing to do. He would never be free to "do his own thing." He would be at the beck and call of his Master 24/7. Paul gladly termed himself a bondservant of God.

As a result, he ended up serving God as an ambassador to the Gentiles. The many letters he wrote that are included in our Bibles are proof that he represented God very well to others. His job, as he expressed it in the letter to Titus, was twofold: to care for the faith of those to whom God sent him, and to represent God's truth accurately.

We are controlled by physical "truths" like the law of gravity and mathematical formulas. We are given "truth" on the evening news and in the classroom. In this age of enforced tolerance, the concept that "truth is relative" assaults us in every area of our lives. If we do not want to lose our footing in life, we must have the right truth as our foundation.

The only way to distinguish *the* truth from counterfeit truth is to examine the results of living by it. "Truth" that says there is no right and wrong eventually leads to anarchy. "Truth" that lowers us to the level of amoral animals destroys hope and causes despair. Only truth that leads to godliness is the right truth. We can simply watch people, and by their life-style we will know if they are following God's truth or some other slippery "non-truth."

Besides giving instruction for believers on how to live godly lives, knowledge of the truth also promotes hope. As you noted at the beginning of this lesson, our world and society is full of sad stories that highlight the futility of life here on earth. Every time an earthquake strikes, a house burns down, a person is killed or dies of illness, God is giving those people touched by tragedy an opportunity to turn to Him for their comfort. Unfortunately, many people shake their fists at the heavens and declare that they want nothing to do with a God who would allow such things. A few recognize God's mercy and swallow their pride, admitting that they cannot go one step further without Him. These will allow God to take the hopelessness of their situation and turn it into hope of eternal life.

This hope is one we can count upon, not like our usual hopes that are merely wishes for things to get better. We can know that our hope in heaven is certain, because God promised it. God, who not only sees past, present, and future but also very carefully controls everything that happens in them, always planned for those who love Him to live eternally with Him. When God plans something, it is not like our plans, which can be thwarted. God's plans will happen.

The book of Titus does not mention trials and tribulations, yet Paul is very careful to prepare the Cretan believers for those experiences by laying this foundation of hope. God is neither surprised nor hindered by the events in our lives. He is very much in charge. When He determines something, it will happen when He wants, how He wants, where He wants, and to whom He wants. It could be very frightening to have a God with so much power if it were not for the fact that He loves us so much. If I am His child (and not just His creature), knowing that eternal life is secure because God, who cannot lie, promised it before time began, comforts me. As we dig into this brief letter, we will discover how this eternal life may belong to us. We will also learn how life here on earth should be lived once we know we have eternal life.

Make Truth Personal

1. List at least four truths we learn about God in this short passage (Titus 1: 1–4).

❧ Pause to Pray ❧

Respond to God "from the heart" about how
these truths affect your life.

---

2. The best way for an ambassador to communicate her President's will to her host country is to know her President well. The better she knows him, the more likely it will be that she can communicate his will accurately.

How can you get to know your Lord better? (See 2 Timothy 3:16–17). How can you change your priorities to make more time to spend with Him?

3. Are you an effective ambassador? To whom does God want you to communicate hope of eternal life? Be specific. Name names. Decide how you can spend more time with these people.

4. Consider 2 Timothy 2:2 and Titus 2:3–5. Do you have a "true child in the faith?" If so, what is your responsibility towards that person? If you don't have a "spiritual child," begin praying about it and ask God to open your heart, your life, and your schedule to someone who really needs Him. Or maybe you'd like to be someone's "Titus." Ask them.

Hope anchors our lives firmly in our certain future,
thus preventing daily shipwreck.

Notes

Session Three
Authority To Lead

Titus 1:5–9

Authority. It's a tricky thing. The more you wield it, the more those "underlings" seem to wiggle out of your grasp. Have you ever tried to hold on to a live, slippery, slimy trout? You're smarter than the fish—and you certainly control its environment—but it has strong muscles. You have to exert just the right amount of pressure to keep it in your hands. Hold it too loosely, and the fish will flop to the ground; too tightly, and it will squirt from your grasp like a bar of wet soap.

Authority used as a means of coercion is not authority at all; it's enforcement. As much as you long to be respected by your children, co-workers, employees, students, or committee members, you can never force them to respect you. You can scream, pout, beg, cry, or faint, but such attempts to control will only drive them to fight more fiercely to remove themselves from your grasp. Exerting dictatorial leadership only proves that you are not a respected authority in that person's life. Authority leads by example.

Look up the word *authority* in your dictionary. According to the many definitions, in what areas of everyday society do we see authority exercised? I have written in an example. List at least three more.

1. *School: Student/Teacher/Administration*

How do people gain authority over others—either legitimately or otherwise? What is the source of their authority? (Who gives it to them?) Write some further examples.

1. *Money: (The giver, or others who wish they could control the wealth)*

Discover God's Truth

Read Titus 1:5–9. Where do the leaders of the local church get their authority?

v. 5: For what two reasons was Titus in Crete?

How was Titus to judge which men to appoint as church leaders?

v. 6: What should be the family responsibilities of an elder? First Timothy 3: 5 explains why.

v. 7: This verse gives us several traits descriptive of a man totally out of control. What would be some indicators that such a man would not be qualified to be a church leader? What would be the opposite of those negatives?

Negatives	Positives

v. 8: What other character traits should a church leader exhibit? Write a brief description or definition of each one. How would these traits be recognized?

v. 9: How does the leader know he is doing what God expects of him?

What are two very important things that a church leader should do for the people in the church?

How will he probably "exhort in sound doctrine"? What will be the basis of his teaching?

How will he know which people need to be refuted? Why would it be good for a church that he does this?

What might happen to a church if the leaders do not refute those who contradict God's Word? (Peek ahead a few verses. More in the next lesson.)

Where does he get the right to do these things?

Fill in the chart on page 32 in the section describing the character traits of godly church leaders.

Paul's little letter to young Titus had a greater purpose than just to instruct and encourage Titus himself. Paul asserted his rank by mentioning his own apostleship in verse 1, and then in verse 5 he gave Titus authority to act on his behalf. The Cretans were to listen to Titus as if Paul had been speaking to them.

In some ways, evangelism and church planting were easier in the first century. The believers went to a town that had never heard the gospel. They preached, and those whom the Holy Spirit convicted of sin decided to change their minds about their former way of life and trust Christ for salvation. They studied the Scriptures for a while until a church was born. The Holy Spirit gave certain men abilities to lead groups of believers and those leaders were eventually officially recognized.

Titus had remained in Crete after Paul left to set in order the things that still needed to be done for that group of believers. First on his list was to recognize the future leaders of each local fellowship on the island. Paul's checklist was explicit and easy to follow.

Make Truth Personal

In our churches today, spiritual authority is often perceived as coming from ordination, commendation, Bible college degrees, seminary diplomas, and fulfillment of academic or social requirements.

1. According to Paul's letter to Titus, where does a church leader get genuine spiritual authority?

Look once more at verse 9. Do you think it would be possible for a man to lose his spiritual authority? How?

While the proper interpretation of this passage deals most specifically with the men[1] who should be leading our churches, we women are certainly free to take the principles and make several applications to our own lives from the godly standards set here.

2. Which character traits do you need to work on? (Naturally you can't be the husband of one wife!) Choose one of those and decide on something that you can do to begin the changing process. Ask God to remind you and help you during the coming week. If you're brave enough, ask a friend to remind you as well.

3. The church is always in need of godly leaders. Who are some of the Christian men in your circle?

❧ Pause to Pray ☙

Pray for your current church leaders to live according to the godly standards set here. (Only pray; do not nag.)

---

4. If you are not married (and would like to be someday), ask the Lord to bring such a godly man into your life. If applicable, pray this for your daughters and granddaughters.

5. Based on #3 above, write a note or letter of encouragement to one of these men, letting him know that his life is an example to you and that you are praying for him. Or you might want to inform your daughter, niece or granddaughter about what kind of a husband you are asking God to provide for her someday.

He who would govern others,
first should be master of himself.
—*Philip Massinger*

Notes

[1] This and several other passages teach that the people in a church who bear the ultimate responsibility for a group of Christians meeting together should be men. They are called pastors, elders, overseers, or bishops in various translations. Clearly, it is impossible for a woman to be a "one-woman kind of man," as Paul taught Titus. See also: 1 Timothy 3:2. The words are not interchangeable.

Character And Deeds Of Godly And Ungodly Leaders
Titus 1:5–16

Leaders/Elders of the Local Church 1:5–9	False Teachers 1:10–16

Session Four
The Dangers Of
Not Knowing The Truth

Titus 1:10-16

**...And it won't make one bit of difference
If I answer right or wrong;
When you're rich, they think you really know.**

— Tevye, from *Fiddler on the Roof*

Nowadays, advice pours over us in avalanches of commercials, articles, television and radio programs, and "expert" testimonies. I could tell you of the junk mail I got just today, offering me improved health, financial well-being, and political wisdom. Sometimes it's hard to know to whom we should listen. Consider these magazine topics:

- "Movie Stars Share Their Mothers' Best Advice." (Do I really want to follow a movie star's mother's advice? Do I want my daughter's life to be like that of a movie star?)
- "19 Smart Ways to Keep Kids Safe." (Safe from what, and what are the author's credentials? It would definitely make a difference whether the article was written by a policeman, an elementary school principal, a New Age guru, or a Christian psychologist.)

- ❧ "Why Gossip is Good for You." (I seem to remember a few Bible verses that say otherwise …)
- ❧ "Natural Remedies: What's Smart, What's Risky?" ("Risky" is probably following any health advice in a woman's magazine. How can we know?)
- ❧ "Stress Makeovers: 3 Paths to Pure Relaxation." (Again, consider the source.)
- ❧ "Nurturing a Child's Pride" (Doesn't the Bible condemn pride?)

List some of the wisdom you get from the magazines you read, TV programs you watch, newspaper articles you quote, Internet sites you browse, and friends you talk with.

If you are honest, this could be very uncomfortable for you. To whom do you listen for advice? How do you evaluate whether you should follow their advice or not? How much do they know about God? Do their opinions, advice, and wisdom agree with or contradict the Bible? How important is that to you?

Discover God's Truth
Look again at Titus 1:9. Name two primary assignments of a godly leader in a local church.

Read Titus 1:10-16 to discover why the elder's job is so important.

v. 10: What sort of people is Paul talking about? Do these people sound as if they are believers in Jesus Christ? What is their religious background?

v. 11: What does Paul think ought to be done to these people? What are they doing wrong? What motivates them?

v. 12: The apostle Paul here quotes from a highly respected Greek poet, Epimenides, who wrote in the sixth century BC. Exceptions surely existed, but his condemnation correctly described this peoples' predominant sins (v. 13). Although probably exaggerated, what were the common characteristics of the Cretans? Could a Cretan become a believer in Jesus Christ and continue to live in these former ways? Explain your answer.

v. 13: What does Paul say about Epimenides' opinion of the Cretans? What should Titus do about it?

Isn't it lacking in love to rebuke someone sharply? Explain your answer.

vv. 13-14: What would Titus hope to accomplish by sharply rebuking these insubordinate idle talkers and deceivers? Name two things that might result. What two things were leading them away from true faith in Jesus Christ?

What happens when believers try to mix their old beliefs with their new faith? What does it do to their testimony?

vv. 15-16: Is it possible for unbelievers to do good works? Explain your answer. See Ephesians 2:8-10.

What are these verses saying, in effect, about the relationship between the motivation of the heart and outward actions? What do good works show about someone who is sincerely seeking God? Does God accept their good works and call them "good?"

Why would these deceivers be unable to communicate the truth to others?

From this passage and a dictionary, describe deceivers. What do they want? How do they get what they want? What are the results of falling under their spell? How can we recognize deceivers?

> ## ❧ Pause to Pray ❧
>
> Ask God to protect your church (and you) from deceivers.
> Ask that He make you wise to recognize them.

Turn to the chart on page 32, "Character Traits of Godly and Ungodly Leaders." Fill in the right hand side related to False Teachers.

❧❧❧

It's embarrassing, isn't it? How easily we listen to the advice of people who are not qualified to give it! And how often we accept the inadequate qualifications of advice-givers!

The reason a local church needs men of integrity and good character to lead it is to protect it. The world is full of charlatans and users who will not even stop at church doors in their quest for more people to mislead and rob. Paul described the Cretan false teachers as rebellious, and then divided them into two categories: empty talkers and deceivers. Idle talkers love to hear themselves talk. They give out information everywhere they go and never doubt that what they have to say is worthwhile—even if it isn't.

Deceivers are, of course, more sinister. Their goal is to convince you not only that their information is worth absorbing, but that their way of life is worth following. They, too, use brilliant rhetoric and the most up-to-date methods. They would be unable to deceive if their goals were not presented in the most attractive packaging.

Deceivers also fall into two categories: those who are themselves deceived, and those who know they are wrong and take a perverse delight in leading others astray. The deceivers Paul mentions here were not trying to destroy Christianity by persecution and oppression. Many Jews to whom Paul preached the gospel accepted that Jesus Christ was, in fact, the Messiah, the Savior of the world. They repented of their sins and gave their lives to Him, becoming believers in Christ. The deceiver, however, knew intellectually who Jesus was and professed faith in Him, but was still trying to make himself acceptable to God by keeping ceremonial laws, rituals, and other man-made commandments.

People who profess Christ but try to fit their old religion and way of life into their new life are probably not genuinely converted. True believers are new creatures who will eventually abandon any practices, superstitions, and rules from their old life that hinder growth in Christ.

Although these people were doing some good works, their motives were wrong. They were still trying to earn favor with God, and we can never do that. Jesus' death on the cross is the only acceptable payment for our sins. Nothing we can do can improve our standing with God. Anyone who says that you must do something to earn God's favor is a deceiver. There is no nice way to express it. Is it any wonder the apostle Paul told Titus to silence these people?

Make Truth Personal

1. Paul agreed with the Cretan stereotype and then told Titus to confront those Cretans who were spreading false teaching. Whether or not you like stereotyping an entire group, you should want to allow God to work to overcome any negative stereotypical nature that you have. Are you part of an identifiable "group"? What sins and weaknesses characterize the groups with whom you associate? What are you doing to overcome them so that they don't hinder your witness for Christ?

2. Look at 2 Corinthians 5:17 and the principle in Matthew 9:16-17. What relationship does an old life without Christ have with a new life in Christ? What things are you holding onto from your old life? What should you do about it?

❧ Pause to Pray ❧

Ask God to open your eyes to areas you need to work on.
Ask His forgiveness for areas you've been neglecting.

---

3. How should we react toward church leaders when they "refute those who contradict" and silence rebellious deceivers? Why? How can you and I support them and show our appreciation?

Perhaps, as you have been doing this Bible study, you are baffled by some of the things you are reading and hearing. Are you trying to change, but becoming frustrated by your slow progress? Have your attempts to clean up your life left you unsure as to whether God accepts you or not? Are you often confused by the variety of teachings you hear? Perhaps you have not yet put your trust in the Lord Jesus Christ. Only He can empower you to make a permanent change, first by forgiving the sins that separate you from God, and then by making it possible for you to glorify Him by your life and deeds. He will open your eyes to understand the Bible and help you see that following Him is the only right way to go.

Following idle talkers will derail you;
following deceivers will wreck your life.

Notes

Session Five
The School Of Good Character

Titus 2:1-10

Character does matter.

As I sat down to write this introduction, a young woman called, asking me to take her to the store. She's a single mom on a limited income, and I have offered to take her shopping at discount stores when she needs to go. She is also a loud, hyperactive, difficult person, the type that uses you, eats up your time, and shows little change for the better (bearing in mind the time and effort you put into her!). I "inherited" this particular "problem person" from a lovely Christian woman who had run out of ideas and patience.

But I am writing a chapter on good works and how those good works can both reveal our godly character and betray our self-centered motives. Good works alone are nothing. Plenty of atheists and God-haters do nice things for people. So whether I take my friend shopping or not is not the issue. The question is: *why* am I taking her shopping?

Part of my reason is efficiency: I won't be able to concentrate on writing until I've settled this. Another part is that I'm a wimp: I have such a hard time saying "no." Part of me feels almost unbearable pity for her unhappy, self-inflicted circumstances. But a little part of me remains for what should be my greatest motivation: God's glory. I know—because I've seen it happen—that God can change the life of even the most difficult person, and I'd like to be around when He changes this one. Then people will really see and know that the Word of God is true!

So pardon me while I take her shopping.

Discover God's Truth

Read Titus 2:1-10. As you read the text fill in the chart at the end of this lesson (you may have a few blanks!)

v. 1: Why does Paul say, "but as for you...."? What is he contrasting? What does he want Titus to do?

v. 2: What are some of the stereotypes of older men? What character traits give evidence that sound, biblical teaching has grabbed the life of an older man? How do these counteract the natural tendencies of older men?

I have a friend who nursed her mother-in-law, then her own mother, and lastly a step-mother, in their final months of life. She observed that the older we become, the more we become like the real "us" inside. That's a scary thought! If you're like me, you don't want people to know what you're really like inside. We need to begin *now* to fill our lives full of God's Word so that when we are old and too tired to maintain the façade we've kept up so long, God's character will flow out of us unhindered.

Because this is a womens' Bible study, we need to take a long look at the natural tendencies that make older women the brunt of so many nasty jokes and ugly sitcoms on television. Name a few of those sinful stereotypes.

v. 3: How important is education, age, rank, and social position for an older woman who wants to teach younger women?

What behavior would God like older women to avoid?

What behavior does God consider necessary for a woman "teaching what is good"?

That little word *likewise* also points back to verse 2, regarding the older men. Add those character qualities to your list as well.

v. 4: Which two major areas should the older women be able to teach?

How will the example of loving one's own husband and children strengthen the older woman's teaching?

v. 5: What character qualities should the older women teach the younger women? List them with a brief description of each.

Did you notice how many of these fly in the face of the Cretans' natural tendencies? Refer back to Titus 1:10-12.

❧ Pause to Pray ☙

Choose a character trait you need to work on and talk to the Lord about it.

What reason does Paul give for the older women to carry out this important assignment? Why would he say this?

We will return to the women, but first, let's finish the paragraph.
vv. 6–7: What unfortunate stereotypes does the world have of young men?

What godly character traits will show the world that this young man belongs to God?

v. 8: How will detractors respond when it becomes evident that the Holy Spirit controls a young man's life?

v. 9: What bad traits would slaves have had to combat? Do we see those same negative tendencies today in employees toward their employers? What character traits does God expect of Christian employees? List them and give a brief definition of each.

What will be the result of an employee's godly conduct in his or her place of employment?

❦

The apostle Paul began chapter 2 with *but* and quickly contrasted the evil deceivers of the previous chapter with young Titus's important assignment. His words were to be "fitting for sound doctrine." When the foundation of a house is sound, it is strong, and can withstand even the weight of a waterbed! When a person's health is sound, there is no need to call the doctor. When an argument is sound, it cannot be refuted, for there are no weaknesses to be corrected.

The issue of sound teaching is an important part of this little letter to Titus, for Paul mentions it twice in the first sixteen verses. If the teaching is sound, the local church will be strong and able, in turn, to feed the individual believers. Sound teaching results in a harvest of good deeds and positive character traits that would be difficult to counterfeit indefinitely. Older men, typically grumpy and inflexible, are to be known for their dignity, love, and strong faith. Older women, stereotyped as having busy tongues, are to busy themselves with training the younger women to live godly lives. Young men, often impetuous and unbridled, are exhorted to be good examples to all. Finally, slaves (and by application, employees), instead of complaining and being lazy, are to be honest and respectful.

Blessed are the people in such a church as this! They honor God's Word and their behavior makes the gospel attractive to all that see it. Consequently, if opponents of the gospel have anything negative to say, they are put to shame, for the believers' good works and sensible living visibly prove that they have built their lives on an unshakeable foundation of sound teaching.

Make Truth Personal

We all have much to learn from one another. Each one of us is an older woman in someone's life, and each one of us is also a younger woman, with something still to learn. We all have experiences with God, gifts from God, and faith in God that we can share with others. We need to avoid the tendencies of assuming we have either nothing to learn or nothing to pass on. We also need to stop making the excuses often used to wiggle out of learning or teaching.

1. Write next to each of the following six excuses what it is that prompts it: is it *pride, self-pity,* or *fear*?

From Older Women:

"No one helped me. Why should I help anyone else?"

"I'm not good enough to offer help to anyone else"

"I have nothing to teach anyone."

From Younger Women:

"I would never dare ask for help."

"I can't find anyone mature enough to teach me"

"I don't think anyone can help me."

2. How do younger women make it difficult for older women to offer their help? When the younger women really would like help, what can they do?

3. Can you think of a younger woman in your church who would be thrilled if you offered to spend time with her in a Bible study, teach her to cook, sew, or keep house? What keeps you from asking her?

4. Can you think of an older woman you admire who would be honored (and maybe a bit embarrassed) if you told her how much you appreciate her and that you'd like to learn from her? What keeps you from doing so?

 Pause to Pray

Pray for a good opportunity to speak to that older/younger woman,
and for the relationship you will build with her.

---

5. Look again at the end of verse 5. What can you do in your family and church to ensure that God's Word is not dishonored? What "private" character trait in your life could dishonor God's Word if it ever became known? What can you do about it now? Ask that dear older lady to help you.

Find a good example;
Follow a good example;
Be a good example;
Be followed.

Healthy Teaching
Titus 2:1-10

People in the Church	Commands Character Qualities Positive and Negative	Reasons to Develop Positive Character Traits and Avoid Negative Ones
Older Men, v. 2		
Older Women, vv. 3-4		
Younger Women, vv. 4-5		
Younger Men, vv. 6-8		
Slaves (employees), vv. 9-10		

Session Six
The Syllabus For "Teaching What Is Good," Part 1

Proverbs 31:10-31

I teach "Ministry of Women" at a Bible college in the Midwest. During the first few weeks of the class the administration requires the faculty to turn in their syllabi. According to Webster's Ninth New Collegiate Dictionary, a syllabus is "a summary outline of a discourse, treatise, or course of study...." In my syllabus I know approximately what I will teach each day. The students know which books to read and when their assignments are due. My syllabus assures that I will cover all the material, putting appropriate emphasis on each topic. At the end of the semester the students evaluate for the administration whether or not the class accomplished what was promised.

If we are going to teach (or be taught) the topics listed in Titus 2:3-5, we need a syllabus. Nowhere in Scripture can we find a more comprehensive list of the admirable qualities of a godly woman than in Proverbs 31:10-31. Just as my syllabus includes only the high points, however, so too these twenty-two verses contain only the topic sentences for many lessons. As we brush past so many different subjects, take note of those you can teach and those you still need to learn.

Proverbs 31:10-31 is an acrostic, in that each verse begins with a successive letter of the Hebrew alphabet. Some commentators believe this acrostic's purpose was to provide a memory device to young women who were just learning how to be wives and mothers. Other scholars point out that the whole book of Proverbs is about God's wisdom for daily life, and as wisdom is personified as a woman in Proverbs, this is the type of woman she would be. Certainly we could do no better than to follow her. Still another view suggests that King Lemuel (mentioned in 31:1) received this list of expectations from his mother when he was old enough to choose a wife. As a mother-in-law myself, I can understand the Queen Mother's high standards, but it would have been a scary list for any prospective bride. This perspective is interesting in that the Queen Mother believed that a future queen should be able to run a household and mend clothing. Since we are thinking of teaching and learning the skills and qualities mentioned in Titus 2:3-5, these verses in Proverbs seem tailor-made for us.

God will give us the strength, abilities, and will to meet these high standards.

Discover the Truth

Read Proverbs 31:10-31.

There is a blank chart at the end of this lesson. While you read these verses again, jot down this capable woman's good deeds and the character qualities that spark them. This second part will take some thought, and you may add to it after Lesson 7. (For example, in verse 16, she considers and buys a field. You might decide that the character qualities that contribute to this are her thrift and good sense.) The third column is to list the opposite of her good traits. These are not actually mentioned in the passage, but because we are sinful people, sometimes looking at the negatives helps us to understand the positives better.

v. 10: How common is it for a man to find a woman like this? Why is she worth more than jewels?

v. 11: Why does her husband trust her? Keep in mind that this trust is much broader than faithfulness in the sexual relationship. In what other areas can he trust her?

How can you tell if a man trusts his wife?

How can that trust be broken?

v. 12: What would it look like if a woman did her husband evil and not good? How bad does something need to be evil? Name some things. What's the extent of the excellent woman's commitment to her husband?

v. 13: What is her attitude to physical work? Must these be her favorite activities?

Name some of the household tasks you do. Which ones are you good at? Which ones are still weak points? Do you know someone who could help you improve?

v. 14: Why would she do this? Why do we look for bargains?

v. 15: This woman has no labor-saving machines, but she does have servants. We sometimes joke about wanting servants, but it is usually because we want someone else to do all the work. What is it like to work for her? Why?

How organized is she? Why would this be necessary?

v. 16: Back in Bible times, where did people get the food and clothing they needed to survive? Why is the field so necessary? How capable is she with the family's finances? Do you think she ever spends more than they have?

v. 17: Some men like weak women. Why would it be so much better for a man to marry a "strong" woman? What sort of strength are we talking about?

v. 18: How does she view her own abilities? What do you learn from that?

Verse 15 says that she rises early. In this verse (18) she works late into the night. What does that say about her?

v. 19: What has she learned to do?

v. 20: What is her relationship to the poor? How does she treat them?

v. 21: Scarlet was another word for the best fabric. In summer, the people probably wore linen, and in the winter, wool. What does this verse say about her care for her family and servants? How would this affect their health?

v. 22: Purple was a very fine fabric often worn by the nobility. Verse 30 says that beauty is vain, yet she clothes herself in fine fabrics. What does that say about how a woman looks and her effect upon those around her? How can we find the balance?

❧ Pause to Pray ☙

Choose one of these verses and pray it for yourself or for a younger woman you know.

This woman is amazing! Are you impressed with her? She seems too good to be true, yet she is in our Bibles for a reason. The man who finds this kind of woman is fortunate indeed. She is a stable rock in his life, making it possible for him to trust her completely. He doesn't have to worry about the finances, upkeep of the house, whether the children will be clothed properly, or what he will eat for supper. In everything she does he can trust her motives, for he knows she is his helper and will always try to do what is best for him, the children, and their home.

She is organized, she doesn't complain, and she knows how to stretch a dollar. She works hard and her hard work just seems to make her stronger. She is unlike the woman who sits around all day watching TV and then complains about being so tired. Laziness not only affects the work that doesn't get done; it also puts a person in a bad mood.

When we do a job well, it is not prideful to see that and be pleased. Yes, humility is precious to God. We all know, however, when our work has been pleasing to those we serve. We recognize success and that recognition guides us to serve others even better. When we are praised for a job well done we need to avoid the false humility of denying the obvious. Give the glory to God, but don't overlook the fact that He helped you accomplish what you set out to do.

One of the things this woman does so well is to care for the physical needs of her family. They are appropriately clothed for the season, they have nourishing food to eat, and the house is clean and organized. Her servants are included in her care, for she recognizes that contented servants will work harder and be more trustworthy. She does not lord it over them just because she holds the checkbook. She finds out what they do best, teaches them what they do not know, and supervises them in a way that communicates acceptance and even love.

When I was in Bible college, I used to get so angry with the guys who overlooked the really quality, godly girls while longing for the empty-headed, beautiful ones. I got frustrated, too with pretty girls who thought they had to dress like frumps, let their hair get stringy, and never use any makeup, thinking this somehow made them seem more spiritual. Well, the Proverbs 31 woman's features may or may not be attractive, but she knows how to dress prettily, and her husband is glad of it.

As you consider how these verses apply to you, remember that you are both a learner and a teacher. Do you have a strong marriage? Find a way to help others to strengthen theirs. Is your housekeeping a constant frustration? Find a woman who excels in that area, and learn from her. Don't let the phrase "excellent woman" scare you off. Everyone excels at something. The trick is to discover what you excel in and teach that. Then work on your weaknesses.

Make Truth Personal

1. Read through these first twelve verses and make a list of household skills a young woman needs to learn before she gets married.

2. How many of these can you teach? How did you learn them? Can you think of a way you could begin to teach a younger woman or two? Perhaps you could invite her over to learn how to cook a special dish. Or you could organize a spring-cleaning team and offer to clean some of your friends' homes. Maybe you could start a sewing class for girls.

3. Name some of the misunderstandings you have with your husband that you know are your fault, but that you would never admit to him. How do these things affect his reliance on you? What can you do about it?

4. Isn't it interesting that simple household chores are considered by God to be good deeds? What turns floor mopping, gardening, toilet cleaning, and cross-stitching into tasks that please God? Look at Colossians 3:17. What should be our attitude as we serve others?

❧ Pause to Pray ❧

Let God know how you'd like to change your attitude.
Humbly ask for His gentle reminders.

---

5. What do 1 Timothy 2:9-10 and 1 Peter 3:3 have to say about our outward appearance? Read these verses carefully. Are we allowed to put any emphasis at all on how we look? What is the most important? Do you need to make any changes?

6. What is your relationship to people who are less well off than you? No matter how poor you think you are, the fact that you live in the West and are participating in this Bible study means that you are richer than most of the people in the world. How can you stretch out your hand to the poor and needy? Read James 1:27.

Charm is deceitful and beauty is vain, but a woman who fears the LORD, she shall be praised. Proverbs 31:30

The Capable Woman of Proverbs 31:10-31

Character Qualities	Good Deeds	Negative Traits to Avoid
10:		
11:		
12:		
13:		
14:		
15:		
16:		
17:		
18:		
19:		
20:		
21:		
22:		
23:		
24:		
25:		
26:		
27-28:		
29:		
30:		

Notes

Notes

Session Seven
The Syllabus For "Teaching What Is Good," Part 2

Proverbs 31:10-31

When I was little, my mother knit wonderful sweaters, mittens, hats, and socks for my sisters and me. She taught me to knit baby booties when I was seven, just before my youngest sister was born. What I remember mostly is being frustrated, for I was trying to follow the rules of knitting without understanding what I was doing. It wasn't until I had small children that I decided to take up the craft again. Knitting is, I guess, a little like riding a bicycle: you never forget how to do it. Only this time, as I looped the yarn around the needle and pulled it through, it made sense. Before long I could adjust sizes, add interesting patterns, and fix mistakes without ripping out the whole piece.

Although I generally knit to utilize time while I'm watching television or riding in the car, it has gradually dawned on me how many hours (and stitches) go into one sweater. A tiny sky-blue cardigan for my two-year-old granddaughter took thirty hours, not counting fixing mistakes. The sweater I made for my 6' 2" son may have taken 150 hours!

Perhaps you do not knit, crochet, or sew. Even so, someone makes your clothes, and the money you use to pay for them takes time to earn. If you buy a sweater for, say, $25, the wage earner in your family would have to work for more than two hours at $12 per hour to pay for it. The point is: acquiring garments to keep us warm and looking nice requires patience and diligence.

The Proverbs 31 woman had it even harder. She had to raise the sheep, supervise their shearing, wash the wool, spin it into thread, weave it into fabric, and sew it into the necessary garments. In verse 25 we read, "Strength and dignity [or honor] are her clothing, and she smiles at the future." As we consider the time invested into clothing ourselves, ask yourself how long it takes to obtain the "clothing" of strength and dignity. Not only that, but why do these things put a smile on her face as she contemplates the future? Let's study.

Discover the Truth

Read Proverbs 31:23-31. Write down any thoughts you have as you read.

v. 23: Why can the husband of this amazing woman enjoy the respect of the community? What does her diligence and efficiency make it possible for him to do?

✣ Pause to Pray ✣

Pray on behalf of all the married women in your church about
supporting their husbands in community involvement.

---

v. 24: How does she supplement the family's income? How much time does she spend away from home to do it?

v. 25: What usually keeps us from smiling at the future?

What are some things about our future that frighten most women?

Answer from the following verses: What is strength? How do we gain strength?

Psalm 46:1:

Isaiah 40:29:

Philippians 4:13:

2 Thessalonians 2:17:

How can God's strength help us not to fear the future?

What is dignity? Some translations say "honor." Look up both words in your dictionary and add the definitions to your glossary. Where does honor usually come from?

Proverbs 3:1-6

Also look at the people she serves: **Proverbs 31: 20, 23, 24, 27, 28:**

As godly women, we will display all sorts of wonderful character traits like honesty, kindness, generosity, and wisdom. People will admire these traits and will see God in us. Proper behavior results directly in others honoring her. Does she seek the honor, or does it come to her as she serves others?

If the future suddenly presents hardship, how can the honor others have for us help us? That is, what will they probably do for us?

v. 26: Read Proverbs 1:7. Where does she get her wisdom?

Whom does she teach? Why don't they feel "put down" by her teaching?

What is the difference between teaching in this way, and nagging?

v. 27: This seems to sum up the physical tasks of this woman. Rewrite this verse in your own words.

v. 28-29: What is her reward for a life of serving everyone she meets? What do her husband and children have to say about her? How would you feel if your family spoke of you in this way?

v. 30: There aren't many sins mentioned in this passage, but in this verse, what are the two she specifically does not commit? Define them.

1.

2.

How long can a woman keep up being "charming?" Why must it end?

How long does true outward beauty last? What causes it to fade? Can we do anything about it?

What is left after the charm and beauty are gone?

v. 31: How does her family know that she fears God? Read Proverbs 1:7 again. What other evidences shout out that this woman is deserving of praise?

One of the most fearful times of my life was when our eldest son came home with his driver's permit. For once my husband was no help, for he put my fears into words: "I feel like there are so many stupid, reckless drivers out there, all aiming their cars right at Erich. He doesn't have the experience to avoid them all."

The future looms over us and can squeeze out our joy—if we let it. Women are especially good at "what ifing" every plan. We want to prevent disaster, humiliation, failure, and inconvenience. This trait makes us perfect for running a household and raising a family, however. After all, we are the ones who know what's for supper because we bought the ingredients last week. We planted the seeds so the tomatoes could be harvested before the frost. We bought winter coats on sale last spring for the children who have grown three inches during the summer. Women anticipate and plan and pave the way. My mother often astounded us with the things she did and knew before we could even ask. "You've got to get up pret-ty early in the morning to get ahead of me!" she would say.

We are also blessed with the ability to see pitfalls and dangers. This is why we hold a toddler's hand when we cross the street. We teach our children instant obedience, so that when we yell, "Stop!" they stop. We insist on washed hands before supper, no roller blades on the stairway, and covering a sneeze. As our children grow older, we teach them the extreme dangers of sexual promiscuity, drug/alcohol use, and reckless driving.

The dark side of all this, however, is the fear our insights produce. These fears can turn us into nags, constantly "reminding" our loved ones of what is best for them. We turn into control freaks, doing and providing, offering and suggesting, until they cease listening altogether. Our fears also cause depression, sleeplessness, overeating, and alienation from those who won't listen to us. Fear cripples us, wiping the smile off our faces and spreading a cloud of gloom over those we love.

The solution is to develop strength that only comes from knowing and trusting God. Personal devotions, studying the Bible with other women, reading good Christian books, and listening to Bible-true preachers and teachers will help us to conquer the fear as we look at things from God's perspective. After all, if God, in His kindness, lavishes even unbelievers with rain and beauty, nourishment and talents, how much more can we count on His faithfulness to us, His own children. Reminding ourselves of how He calmed our fears in the past can help. God gives us strength; we must use it.

The other thing that can bring our fears under control is our relationships with other people. As we selflessly serve others, we are unconsciously developing a base of grateful friends who would do anything to help us if disaster strikes. My husband and I were missionaries in Austria for fifteen years and, as a result of our ministry, dozens of people came to know the Lord Jesus as their Savior from sin. One of the scariest things about leaving there was giving up all those friends who supported and encouraged us. Although we have been gone now for several years, I know that, if I needed them, they would help me. This is how honor helps us to smile at the future.

The Proverbs 31 woman is not motivated by her desire to be honored and praised. When her husband and children express their admiration and appreciation, she is surprised, because she is not aware that anyone has been paying any notice. As Colossians 3:17 suggests, she is busy doing what she ought to do with an attitude of serving God.

Make Truth Personal

1. Describe a dream that your husband, father, or grown brother has. Is there anything you need to do to get your life in order so you are not hindering him?

Do people admire him or feel sorry for him because of you?

2. What are things you fear about the future? How do you react when things go wrong or when trials come?

❧ Pause to Pray ☙

Ask God to remind you of this lesson the next time you are tempted to be fearful about the future. Ask for strength to trust Him.

How can you begin to "sew" yourself a garment of strength and dignity? Write down one thing you can do this week to strengthen your relationship with God.

3. Read Proverbs 1:7 again. Where does she get her wisdom?

4. How much time do you spend each day on personal hygiene and outward beautification (including shopping for make-up, going to the beauty salon, and browsing magazines on weight loss)?

Could you begin now to spend at least equal time in getting to know God better? Think about it.

Through many dangers, toils, and snares
I have already come;
'Tis grace that brought me safe thus far,
And grace will lead me home.
—Isaac Watts

Notes

Session Eight
Amazing Grace

Titus 2:11-14

I have heard that if you were to stand at the bottom of a very deep well, you'd be able to see the stars—even in the middle of the day. Of course I have never done it. I expect it has something to do with contrast. Everyone knows that the darker the night, the brighter the stars. True astronomers seek the tops of secluded mountaintops on which to build their telescopes. There, far from city lights, high above smog and dust, the heavenly bodies shine more brightly when their backdrop is the blackest heaven.

In a spiritual sense, unregenerate people live in darkness. In John 3:19 we read of those who "loved darkness rather than the light because their deeds were evil." Unlike astronomers, who guard their darkness so they can better enjoy and study the stars, sinners live in darkness because they enjoy the things they do there. They do not want light to shine on them, for then they would have to face the sinfulness of the things they are doing. God loved us, however, and shined the light of His grace into our dark world.

Before we took a detour to Proverbs 31, we had read Paul's instructions to Titus regarding how sensible people who receive sound teaching act in a healthy church. In this passage Paul gives reasons to obey that cannot be ignored. Our behavior is directly linked to God by His grace. Initially, that grace made salvation available to all. God's grace is a salvation-bringing grace.

The effect of this grace can be seen in good deeds and positive character traits that are not easy to counterfeit indefinitely. It is a grace that instructs us how to live right now in the 21ST century, and then gives us the strength to do it. And finally, this grace looks forward to our future in heaven, giving us hope to persevere when things are difficult. Amazing grace!

Discover God's Truth
Read Titus 2:11–14. What has God's grace done for His children?

Pause to Pray

Praise and worship God for the things He has done for you.

Name some things God expects from us.

Using a good dictionary, find the definitions for the following words and fill in your glossary.

Hope:

Redeem:

Purify:

Zealous/Eager:

v. 11: What has appeared? Check your glossary for the definition. To whom has it appeared?

vv. 11–12: God's grace appears as a sudden bright star in our dark world of sin. What two things does God's grace teach us?

v. 12: What can we learn from God's grace? That is, what do we un-learn and what do we learn?

Look up *deny* in the dictionary.

How do we deny ungodliness and worldly behavior?

What do we find difficult about applying these things in our "present age"?

v. 13: What is our greatest motivation as we try to live a life pleasing to God?

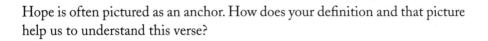
Hope is often pictured as an anchor. How does your definition and that picture help us to understand this verse?

Whose sudden bright appearing gives us hope?

v. 14: What did Jesus Christ do for us? Why?

From what did He redeem us? Who owned us before?

Did we clean ourselves up to make us acceptable to Him? Who did the purifying? To what purpose?

How eager should we be to serve Jesus Christ?

When the first tiny ray of God's grace blinds us, we shield our eyes from the pain. We have lived in the darkness too long. At that point, we make a choice: do we squeeze our eyes closed or do we dare to wish to see more? God's grace shines like a blinding star against the backdrop of our wickedness. His grace makes salvation available to everyone, but only those who step into His light will benefit. They will suffer the pain of seeing their sin as it really is, but to a good purpose: His grace is a salvation-bringing grace.

It is also an instructing grace. Saving people was not enough for God. He also wanted to make us into clean and useful creations, capable of goodness, kindness, purity, love, and humility. He knew these things would be beyond our ability, even after He saved us. So He continues to work painstakingly and patiently with us through His grace.

The instructions of His grace are two-fold. First, it shows us how to deny ungodliness and worldly desires—to turn our back on them—because at their root are the lies that Satan wants us to believe. If we embrace them we will not be able to grasp the second thing that God's grace enables us to do: to be sensible, righteous, and godly. While we are cleaning out the old, we are letting God's grace bring in the new.

Lastly, God's grace is forward-looking. It does not just save us from our sinful past and fix what is wrong with us now. It also looks forward to eternity and gives us a sense of expectancy about the future when the glory of Jesus Christ will appear before our eyes. We will finally see the one who made it possible for us to receive so much grace from the Father. He is the one who paid the price to free us from the deeds that did not please God. His death purified us, as gold is purified by removing the dross. We became His prized possession.

Now we not only have been given the capacity by His grace to do deeds that please God, we actually look forward to doing them. We are eager to go on to the next good deed, for we are no longer doing them in hope of increasing God's favor. We have been given a passion to live according to the salvation-bringing, goodness-instructing, forward-looking grace that has shone into our lives.

Make Truth Personal

1. In verse 12 Paul tells what God's grace teaches us. What are the two unprofitable things we are to say "no" to? Are these things active or passive? That is, do we consciously decide to do them, or do we do them naturally?

2. What are some things that are ungodly in your life? What worldly desires do you struggle with?

❧ Pause to Pray ✺

Tell God how much you want the struggle to end. Ask for His enabling grace to help you change.

---

3. What are the positive things that God's grace teaches us? Are these active or passive? Give some practical examples of each.

4. What would change in your life if you allowed God's grace to teach you these things?

5. Who is it that brings about such change? What has He done for you? Is that enough? What can you do for Him? Where do you get the ability?

These are good verses to memorize, for they are encouraging and motivating. I printed them out and stuck them to my bathroom mirror until I knew them. Memorizing with friends is a great support activity. Hiding God's Word in our hearts gives the Holy Spirit more to use in transforming our lives.

Practice living according to God's salvation-bringing, goodness-instructing, forward-looking grace.

Session Nine
"There, But For The Grace Of God, Go I"

Titus 2:15-3:7

Nero. Hitler. Stalin. Their very names evoke horror, portraying, as they do, all that is the most evil in human nature. How could these men face themselves in the mirror? How could they eat with those bloodied hands? How could they kiss their children good night?

Paul knew about that depth of wickedness, for he lived in Nero's time. The Roman Emperor, Claudius had adopted Nero, so that he (Claudius) could have control over who would be the next Caesar. Nero's stepmother (wife of Claudius) hastened events by poisoning her husband. Traditional stories say that Nero burned a large section of Rome and then blamed it on the Christians. No one knows if this is true, but about the same time a great persecution of the Christians was unleashed. Nero was able to build his Golden Palace in place of the homes and markets that had been destroyed by the fire.

Most of us are not as evil as Nero. We are not even as cruel as Paul was before his conversion. Our sins may seem small and petty by comparison. They are easy to excuse, for everyone does them. They spring, however, from a heart that is "deceitful above all things and desperately wicked" (Jeremiah 17:9).

I came face to face with my own evil heart when I was ten years old. There were many sins I had never committed; in fact, there were sins I didn't even know *were* sins. I was, however, as naughty as I could be, considering my strict parents. I lied, I sassed my mother, I stole cookies, and I even stole candy from the local drug store. When the Holy Spirit finally showed me that Jesus Christ had died on the cross for these things, I dissolved in tears. I had no choice but to ask Him for His mercy and forgiveness and to give Him my little, insignificant life. He forgave me and made my life significant by showing me how to please Him.

Discover the Truth

v. 15: The "these things" in Paul's command here could refer to what he has already said in chapter 2, or what he is about to say in chapter 3, or both. We are going to treat it as a new section. What does Paul tell Titus to do? Name the three verbs. What nuances do each of these have?

1.

2.

3.

In what mode was Titus to do these things: apologetically, gently, or how? What does that say about their importance?

Who was excluded from these instructions?

What do you conclude was the attitude he expected of those receiving these instructions?

v. 1: What should be the attitude and behavior of the believers toward those in political authority over them?

The Romans had conquered Crete and made it a Roman province in 66 BC. The book of Titus was written around AD 65, over one hundred years later. The Romans were, therefore, the rulers and authorities at that time.

Drawing from your general knowledge, (A) how did the Romans become rulers, and (B) what kind of rulers were they?

What is usually our attitude toward ungodly authorities? What is Paul's instruction to the Cretan believers? Are there any exceptions? Read Acts 4:18-20.

v. 2: What else should the believers do?

❧ Pause to Pray ❧

Pray for those in authority over you who do not know the Lord Jesus.

---

v. 3: Why should we have such attitudes and behavior towards those who seem so evil? (What were we like before we met Jesus Christ?) Is this verse a good description of Emperor Nero?

v. 5: We all have the capacity to be as evil as Nero was. What has happened to prevent believers from becoming like him?

v. 4: Why would God do this? (What was His motivation?)

v. 5: What could not save us? On what basis has God saved us?

vv.5–6: According to these verses, what is the role of the Holy Spirit in salvation?

v. 7: What is the result of us being saved according to God's mercy? (See v. 5).

What part do good deeds play in verses 5–7? Why are good deeds important in verse 1? What is the difference?

v. 7: What is an heir? What is the final hope for people who have been justified by God's grace? How certain is this? Look back at Titus 1:2.

If you remember, Paul informed Titus in 1:10-11 that the church will always harbor a few undesirables. He was very clear on who they are, calling them rebels, empty talkers, and deceivers. These are the cult leaders, the founders and perpetrators of false religions, old and new, who have lied their way into the church. They twist truth, perverting the message of the gospel of Jesus Christ to include falsehood as well. They are "spin-meisters," willfully misunderstanding and distorting the Truth. Paul wants Titus to silence them, for their talk fills the air with sound, though they have nothing worthwhile to say. All they do is stir up trouble.

In contrast, Paul wants Titus to speak, exhort, and reprove with all authority. Titus has much to say that is worthwhile, and it is all based upon God's revealed truth. With each phrase in Titus 2:15, Paul gives Titus more and more right to be the one voice that will influence the spiritual life of the Cretan church for years to come.

First, Paul tells him to *speak*; his message was not "empty talk," but important instruction that he was responsible to convey with his lips. Second, Titus was to *exhort*, a stronger term, indicating that there was an aspect of warning to the content of his teaching. Next, Paul tells him to *reprove* the believers if necessary, meaning to scold and correct them. Not only that, but he was to correct them with a commanding attitude of authority, even though he was probably younger than some of them. Finally, Paul says, "Let no one disregard you."

What could be so important? We expect the next verse to include great things we are to do for God. Instead, we receive a reminder to obey the rulers and authorities. We must remember that Paul knew what these rulers and authorities were: ungodly, perverted, and murderous toward true believers. Yet the Cretan Christians were ordered to obey them. Not only that, but their first tendency in every situation should be to do a good deed.

Further, in spite of the despicable life style of the authorities, the believers were told not to malign anyone. Maligning is different from slander. Slander makes up lies to ruin a person's reputation. When we malign someone, we put a negative spin on what the person is doing, whether good or bad. Maligning includes assuming that their motives are bad, that they are deliberately causing problems, and that they could do something about it if they only tried hard enough.

Sometimes we forget that we were once just like them. When we were unsaved, with unchanged hearts, we could not help our evil behavior. Do we really believe that? Let's make this truth more personal.

Make Truth Personal

Many things that our local and national political and economic leaders are currently doing fly in the face of biblical standards. Sometimes it's difficult not to feel angry and discouraged. We want to straighten people out, or at least alert them to the danger to their soul.

Additionally, the media and well-meaning friends can put a more negative spin on these things. For example: "That senator wants poor children to die!" is a maligning comment. No matter how incomprehensible the senator's philosophy and policies seem to be, he, of course, obviously does not want children to die.

1. What should be our attitude and behavior toward sinful, unbelieving authorities?

Name the people who will benefit from your unusual viewpoint. How?

2. What in our past should give us more understanding of the failings of our political leaders?

Our world today insists we must tolerate any and all life styles and choices that others make. How can we obey verses 1 and 2 without giving the impression that we condone their sinful behavior?

3. What do you think should happen when the person described in verse 3 meets the person in verses 4–7? Which one has the resources to understand what is really going on? Has the power to change? Has the ability to love and forgive without condoning sin?

❧ Pause to Pray ❧

Thank and Praise God for what He's done for you. Ask Him to show you how to respond to people in verse 3.

4. Name someone in your life who holds some authority over you. What needs to change in your speech and behavior that will let others see more clearly that you are the person in verses 4–7? (Perhaps you cannot answer this question because you are still the person in verse 3. If so, go on to the next question.)

5. Look at Titus 3:5. Can man in his natural state ever be good enough to please God?

How does God save us?

Read again verses 3–7. If you give your life to God, what will you lose? What will you gain? Perhaps you could talk to your Bible study leader about this.

Although you weren't as bad as you could have been, only God's grace kept you from becoming worse than you could ever imagine.

Notes

Kitchen Table Studies

Session Ten
Good Deeds Meet Needs

Titus 3:8–15

In her mid 1980's hit song, Bette Midler sang, "God is watching us from a distance." She imagined how the earth would look from outer space: a blue and white globe of environmental purity. The residents of this globe, tapping into their inborn decency, would live in harmony. No wars would mar the landscape; no nuclear mushroom would push through the sparkling white clouds. God, that great, white-bearded grandfather in the sky, would sit back in contentment and watch us put our goodness to work.

Most people believe in God. When pressed, even atheists will admit that they have not gathered enough experiences in life to state emphatically that there is no God; if God exists, He's too far away to be of any significance or benefit to anyone.

But God is not "watching us from a distance." He not only sees the deeds and hears the words of every human being, He "sees" right into each heart and "hears" each motivation. We mortals can't bamboozle Him into thinking we are good. Before we're saved, even our most noble deeds are tainted with pride and ambition, and no amount of good deeds can ever outweigh our sins. What "saved" us was that God really *wanted* to save us. He loved mankind so much that His kindness became an unstoppable force. But He could not just pat us all on the head and overlook our sins; His holy anger still had to be satisfied.

So He poured it all out upon His own beloved Son, Jesus Christ, and judged Him in place of us.

Paul described the Cretan Christians at this point as "those who have believed God" (3:8). *They* knew God wasn't a distant deity. He had taken extraordinary steps to come up close and personal. They had taken Him at His word, been justified by His grace, and by means of a God-given make-over been changed from lazy good-for-nothings into people with a purpose.

We 21ST century believers have been given the same "God's eye view" on deeds as those 1ST century ones. With His Spirit living in us, we can steer our attitudes and motivations into service that is good and profitable for everyone. Unlike our old "good" deeds, which were attempts to make ourselves look good while helping others, these good deeds truly please God.

Discover the Truth

v. 8: Once more we have a break in thought, as Paul speaks directly to Titus. What does Paul want Titus to do? What is his reason?

What is the use of good deeds? Whom do they help?

❧ Pause to Pray ☙

Ask God to show you some good deeds you could do to meet true needs among unbelievers.

---

v. 9: What are these people doing? What is the use of these things?

v. 10: What do all of these petty arguments cause in the church? How should the leaders of a church deal with such people? Some translations say we should avoid these types of people, but the original word says to reject them. Isn't that a bit harsh?

Read Matthew 18:15–20. What does Jesus say is the procedure for handling one of His followers who does not repent of a sin?

v. 11: Why are the leaders justified in treating a factious man in such a sharp manner? What do they know about him?

Why would it be good for the church leaders to protect the people in the church in this way? Remind yourself of Titus 1:10–11 and 14 for more insight.

What is the difference between the people in verses 3:1–3 and the ones here in verses 10–11 that explain the way these people are to be handled?

Finally, Paul wraps up this little letter with greetings and personal instructions to Titus and the believers on Crete.

v. 12: What do you think Artemas or Tychicus would be doing while Titus visited Paul at Nicopolis during the winter? Read Ephesians 6:21–22 and Colossians 4:7–9. Tychicus was one of the young men who traveled and evangelized with Paul. What type of a person was he? What benefit would he be to the Cretan Christians?

v. 13: Apparently, Zenas and Apollos were visiting Crete, perhaps preaching in the churches or evangelizing in the cities. The Bible says nothing more about Zenas, but turn now to Acts 18:24–28 and read how Apollos came to Christ. What kind of a person was Apollos? What would the Cretan churches gain from his ministry?

What does Paul want Titus and the believers to do for these servants of God? How much help were they to give Paul's helpers?

v. 14: What must all believers learn to do? What kinds of needs do you think Paul was talking about? Why should the believers meet these needs?

When something doesn't come naturally, we need to be trained to do it. Looking back at the whole book of Titus, but most particularly at chapter 2, how do believers teach other believers to do good works?

Although Crete was a tiny island in the middle of the Mediterranean Sea, the believers there seemed to have their fair share of every kind of unbeliever in their community. In the previous section we looked at the unbelieving political and civic leaders who made life difficult for the believers. Paul urged the believers to resist their natural tendencies to grumble and rebel. Instead, they were encouraged to submit to their rulers' authority and to be gentle and understanding towards them. How unexpected that behavior must have been to all who witnessed it!

Paul had less tolerance for unbelievers who had sneaked their way into the communities of believers. As we saw in 1:10–16, one of the easiest ways to recognize them was to observe the turmoil they caused among the families in the congregations. Paul's teaching (which was God's revelation) was not enough for them. They supplemented it with outdated Jewish traditions, picky man-made legalisms, hearsay, and irrelevant rabbit trails. They were obviously troublemakers who thrived on causing strife. Instead of quietly doing good deeds that would prove whether their teachings were true or not, they concentrated on arguments and disputes that Paul called unprofitable and worthless.

Most everyone has views on some feature of church life and practice that the Bible doesn't even address. Maybe it is what is proper to wear to church, or how communion is organized, or which songs are the appropriate ones to sing at a particular meeting. Many churches have split over such topics. We have been doing certain things for so long, and they are so comfortable, that they must be "right." We feel more spiritual when we do them; surely others would feel the same if they would only try it our way? The problem is when traditions and man-made commandments become the subject of disputes and controversies. Although the issues themselves are not necessarily unprofitable and worthless, the resulting disruption within a congregation *is*.

What we need is a good test to determine whether we are defending an unshakeable truth of Scripture, or merely enjoying a tradition that the Bible doesn't expressly say is either right or wrong. Try asking yourself if believers in other countries practice these kinds of things: baptism, celebrating the Lord's Supper, evangelizing, studying the Bible, male leadership in the local church. These are all non-negotiables, for the Bible teaches them very clearly. What the Bible does not tell us is the nitty-gritty how-tos. Each congregation, in each culture, and in each generation, must decide these.

When you find yourself expecting others to follow a tradition you like, determine whether or not you really have scriptural support for it. Could it just be your opinion, supported by years of tradition? As believers filled with the Holy Spirit, we do not want to be the ones who are stirring up strife and unhappiness. In John 13:35, Jesus told His disciples, "By this all men will know that you are My disciples, if you have love for one another." The one place we should be able to go to enjoy sweet, conflict-free relationships is the meetings of the local church. If this is not the case, something needs to be done.

Paul gave Titus advice that very few church leaders today ever take. He said to reject a divisive person after two warnings. The remedy seems so harsh; yet many churches suffer from chronic strife because the leaders spend too much time trying to reason with troublemakers. People like this, however, do not listen, for deception is by nature unreasonable. Paul equates their refusal to back down as perverted and sinful. They are rebellious (1:10), because they themselves want to be the authority.

As women in a local church, we probably do not have much to do with controlling troublemakers. We can, however, support the leaders by praying for discernment and wisdom in their personal dealings with these people. Our attitude, actions, and words can encourage or discourage the leaders as they labor through these difficult decisions. Instead of wondering why the leaders are so mean and intolerant, we should thank them for following God's Word and for watching out for the welfare of the entire church. Our churches would be more peaceful if the leaders rejected a factious person after two warnings, and if the rest of the believers would not gossip about the inadequacies of their leaders.

Leading a church is hard work, and even leaders need a little rest and recuperation. Paul wanted to make sure Titus got some. In the conclusion to his letter he invited Titus to spend the winter with him. This would surely have been an encouragement to Titus—rather like attending a conference to replenish spiritual strength. Paul, aware of continued needs in Crete, planned to send a man to help out in Titus's absence. Artemas is not mentioned anywhere else in Scripture, but we can assume that he was just as good a man as Tychicus, whom Paul described as a beloved brother and a faithful minister in the Lord who would comfort the hearts of the people wherever he went. The Cretan Christians would certainly benefit from good Bible teaching and lots of comfort brought by someone Paul knew well.

The letter Titus held in his hand had been brought to him by two of Paul's fellow workers: Zenas the lawyer and Apollos. Again, we know nothing more about Zenas, but Apollos was a powerful teacher. Titus could relax, knowing that troublemaking deceivers would be no match for the authority that Apollos brought from his knowledge of God's Word.

Make Truth Personal

1. Write down some of your religious traditions and preferences. (Perhaps you consider jeans unsuitable for church meetings, or you favor the old hymns.) If "push came to shove" over that issue, challenge your heart with what would be most important to you: your tradition or unity in your church?

2. How can you support your church leaders when they feel it is necessary to discipline or even reject a troublemaker?

❧ Pause to Pray ❧

If this is currently happening in your church, pray for your leaders. If it isn't, thank God and pray for protection.

---

3. What good deeds can you personally do to meet pressing needs among the believers in your church?

4. Write a short comparison between the people in verses 9–11 and the friends of Paul in verses 12–13. Compare their deeds, their motives, and the fruit of their lives.

Do all the good you can,
In all the ways you can,
In all the places you can,
At all the times you can,
To all the people you can,
As long as ever you can.
—John Wesley

Session Eleven
Motivated By Hope

A bumper sticker on an RV reads: "I'm spending my children's inheritance." The fanciful first line of a last will and testament says: "I, John Doe, being of sound mind and body, spent it all." In Charles Dickens' novel *Great Expectations*, a twist of fate provides the young hero with an inheritance from a most distasteful source. In fact, many of the great stories of classic literature involve conflicts over the acquisition and division of an inheritance.

When we inherit something—whether it is just Great-Aunt Tilly's carnival glass vase or ten thousand dollars from our parents—one thing is always true: it is not something we earned. The inheritance has been put in place by someone else's hard work, and if I inherit it, it's only because of the foresight and good will of the person who has chosen to favor me after they die. I can do little more than show kindness and respect to my benefactor.

In Luke 10:25–28 a religious expert approached Jesus and asked what he supposed to be a tricky question: "Teacher, what shall I do to inherit eternal life?" His question was a good one, and showed he understood that eternal life can only be inherited. He wanted, however, to do something. Like a fortune-seeking grandson, he wanted to "butter up" the one bestowing the inheritance. He wanted a formula to increase his chances of receiving eternal life.

Jesus, forcing the man to think the issue through, countered with another question. "What is the answer you already know?" would be a way to express it, for the man was a scholar of God's Law and really had no need to ask the question at all.

The answer should come as no surprise, for what wealthy father would want to leave his inheritance to an ungrateful, unloving, unkind child? "You shall love the Lord your God with all your heart, and with all your soul, and with all your strength, and with all your mind; and your neighbor as yourself." The only condition for receiving the inheritance is love for the One who would be providing it. The work has already been done. The inheritance is certain. Only the identity of those who will receive it is uncertain, and the "conditions" placed on them are not really conditions at all. The Father is going to lavish an inheritance on every one of His children. Who are His children? They are recognized by their obvious love for God that is made visible by their ability and willingness to love others. Notice that, after telling the man the parable of the Good Samaritan (Luke 10:29–37), Jesus didn't answer his question as to who his neighbor was. Instead, he asked, "*Who proved to be a neighbor* to the man who fell into the robbers' hands?" After grudgingly admitting it was the one who had shown compassion, Jesus said, "Go and do the same." The love does not earn the inheritance; the love is merely the proof that they really are the Father's children.

Discover God's Truth

To finish the book of Titus, it seems appropriate to once more consider an overview of it. Now that you know the contents so much better, let's summarize some of the main topics.

1. Look at the following verses. Besides all the things Titus was told to teach the Cretan church, what were Paul's personal words to him? What did Paul want Titus himself to do and to be?

1:4–5:

1:13:

2:1:

2:15:

3:8:

3:12–13:

What do these say about using authority to maintain control in a local church?
Do you think Titus was a dictator? Give reasons for your answer.

```
╭─────────────────────────────────────────────╮
│            ❧ Pause to Pray ❧                  │
│                                               │
│   Ask God to make you gracious toward those   │
│      over whom you have authority.            │
│                                               │
╰─────────────────────────────────────────────╯
```

The subtitle of this study book is *Sound Teaching, Sensible Living, and Good Deeds*. In the following three sections, list the verses that mention these three subjects, and summarize what you have learned about each.

Sound Teaching (or Doctrine):

Sensible Living:

Good Deeds:

Find the three sections (one in each chapter) that discuss in detail what God has done for humankind. Summarize what they reveal about God's character and what He has done. Notice particularly that the word "hope" occurs in all three paragraphs. What place does "hope" have in each one?

⊱⟡⟡⊰

We usually use the word hope in contexts of uncertainty.

- ⊱ "I hope my grandchildren can come for Christmas" means it would be really nice, but we'll have to wait to see if it can be arranged.
- ⊱ "I hope you have a good day" is simply a good luck wish.
- ⊱ "I hope I'm going to heaven" implies no one can possibly know whether they will or not.
- ⊱ "I hope I can do enough good deeds to please God" bases my hope squarely on my own abilities, which are changeable and finite.
- ⊱ "I hope that when I die, God will see how much I tried to please Him. After all, 'God is love'" communicates a reliance on an emotional God whose heart will soften when He sees me.

In this kind of hope there is always an undercurrent of optimism, as if keeping a positive attitude will somehow make everything turn out right.

While attitude is very important to how we do things, it doesn't necessarily affect or control the outcome. Sincerity will not convince God to close His eyes to the fact that I do not belong to Him. No one ever pleased God by sincerity alone, and I could be sincerely wrong. No matter how sincere I am, the only way to receive eternal life is to inherit it. It is a gift that comes with becoming a child of God through faith in His Son's work on the cross. I can only come to God His way.

Biblical hope is a firm confidence about the future based on what God has promised His children. We began this study of Titus by considering how Paul and Titus' lives were supported and given purpose by their hope of eternal life. Strengthened by this certainty, they were able to pour themselves into the lives of others. They had no need to worry about their future, for God had already provided that. They could not lose their eternal life by anything they did or did not do, for they had done nothing to earn it. They did not have to "watch out for themselves," because God was going to take care of them now and forever. They had been freed to serve others with a reckless abandon that would astonish anyone watching. Only a rock-solid confidence in the future could do that.

Make Truth Personal

1. How can you increase your intake of sound teaching? Why would you want to? Whom would it benefit?

2. What are some areas in your life that are out of control? Whom can you learn from?

Is there anyone to whom you need to be teaching sensible living? How much does your example and lifestyle matter? What can you do about it?

3. Name some of the things that keep you from doing good and helping others. What thought processes usually give you an "out"?

Check your glossary for the definition of *zealous*. When people see us doing good deeds, what unusual characteristics should describe our way of doing them?

4. Turn back to the first lesson and look at the questions you wrote after a first reading. Has your study of the book answered them? If you're still confused about one, ask a church leader to help you. That's what the leaders are for: "to exhort in sound doctrine."

5. In this study we have dug deeply into what it means to have a certain hope of eternal life. How has this knowledge changed your thinking about things that happen to you? How can this future hope influence your life each day?

And now, LORD, for what do I wait? My hope is in You.
Psalm 39:7

Glossary

Apostle

Deeds/Works

Dignity

Doctrine/Teaching

Faith

Good/Goodness

Grace

Honor

Hope

Purify

Redeem

Self-controlled

Sensible

Strength

Truth

Zealous/Eager

Notes

Notes

Notes

Notes

Also available from
ECS Press
(A division of ECS Ministries)
PO Box 1028
Dubuque, IA 52004-1028
(888) 338-7809
ecsorders@emmaus.edu